Body Books

Bones

Anna Sandeman
Illustrated by Ian Thompson

COPPER BEECH BOOKS
BROOKFIELD, CONNECTICUT

Copyright © 1995 Aladdin Books Ltd.
Produced by
Aladdin Books Limited
28 Percy Street
London W1P 9FF

Designed by David West
Children's Book Design
Designers: David West, Flick
Killerby
Photography: Roger Vlitos
Picture Research: Brooks Krikler
Research
Consultants: Dr. R. Levene, M.D.
Jan Bastoncino, Dip. Ed.

First published in Great Britain in 1995
by Watts Books, London

First published in 1995
in the United States by
Copper Beech Books,
an imprint of
The Millbrook Press
2 Old New Milford Road
Brookfield, Connecticut 06804

Printed in Belgium

1 3 5 4 2

ISBN
1-56294-621-8 (lib. bdg.)
1-56294-639-0 (pbk.)

CIP data is on file at the Library of
Congress.

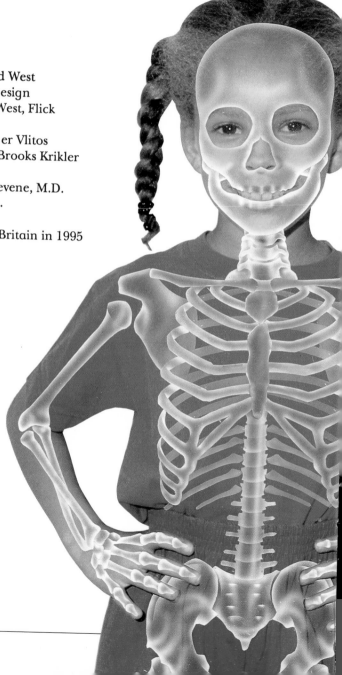

Contents

Who has bones? 6

What are bones? 8

The human skeleton 10

The spine 12

The skull 14

Fingers, hands, and arms 16

Legs, feet, and toes 18

Joints 20

Muscles 22

Growing 24

Broken bones 26

Did you know? 28

Index 30

Who has bones?

Every kind of animal has its own special shape. All animals, including you, can only keep their shape because their bodies are supported in some way. A fully-grown human is held together by over 200 bones.

All bones fit together neatly to form a skeleton inside the body.

Running down the center of the human skeleton is the backbone, or spine. Animals with backbones, including birds, reptiles, and fish, are called vertebrates.

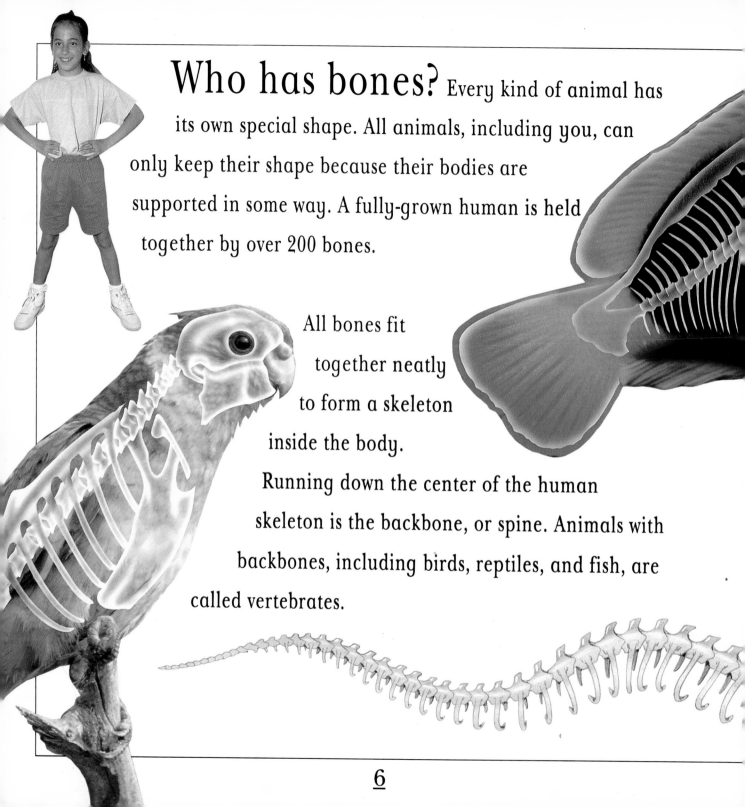

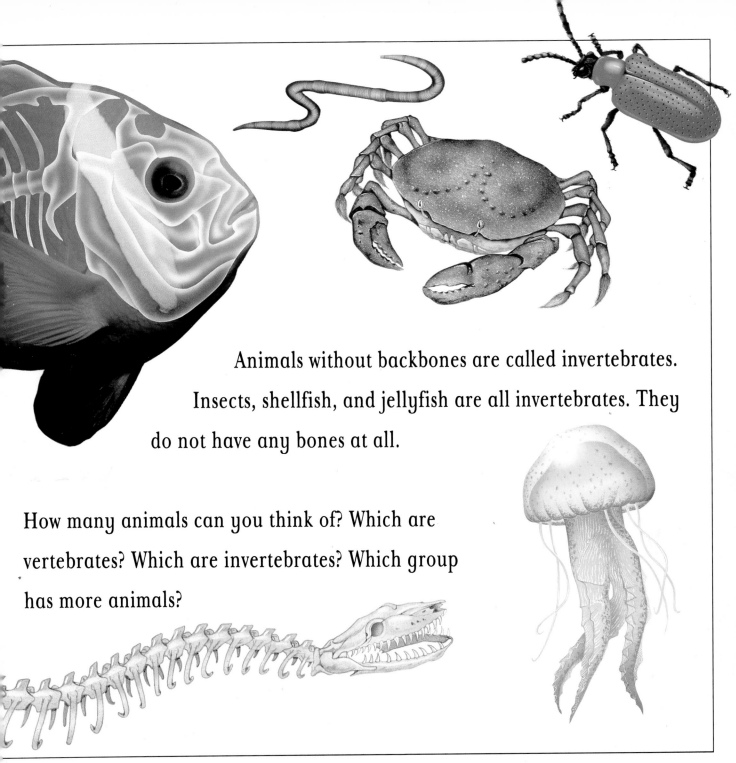

Animals without backbones are called invertebrates. Insects, shellfish, and jellyfish are all invertebrates. They do not have any bones at all.

How many animals can you think of? Which are vertebrates? Which are invertebrates? Which group has more animals?

What are bones?

Some people think bones are just brittle, dried-up, stick-like things. In fact, living bones are just as much alive as the rest of you. Throughout your life they keep growing and changing shape to give your body the support it needs.

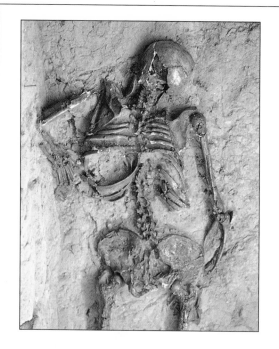

This skeleton is over 1,000 years old. Your bones are very different from these.

What would you look like without any bones?

Bones are made up of different parts.

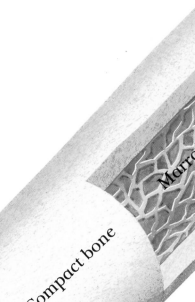

Compact bone

Marrow

The outer part of the bone is smooth and hard. This is called compact bone. The inner part looks more like a sponge, and is called spongy bone.

Spongy bone

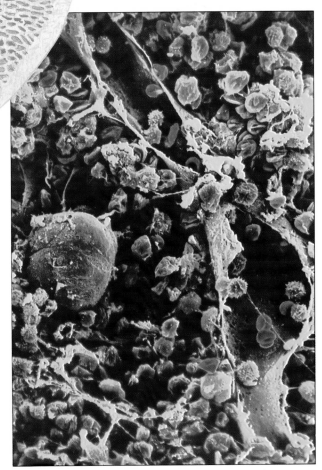

Spongy bone is lighter than compact bone, but still hard and strong.

Inside many bones is a fatty jelly called bone marrow. This is where most of your blood cells are made.

You can see the blood cells in this magnified picture of bone marrow.

The human skeleton

When you were born, you had over 300 bones. They were very soft. They were made of a kind of gristle, called cartilage, as well as firmer bone. As you began to develop, the cartilage hardened into bone and some bones grew together. This will go on happening until you become a fully-grown adult. By that time you will have just over 200 bones, although you will be more than three times the height you were at birth!

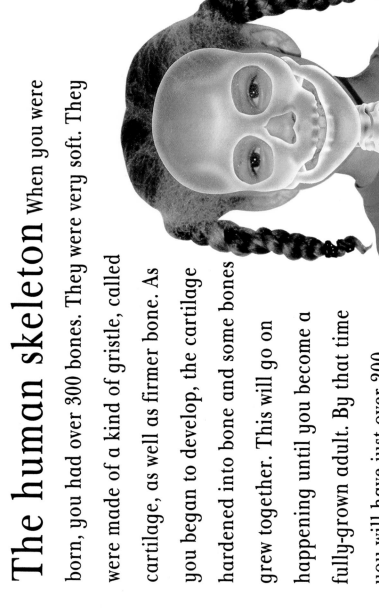

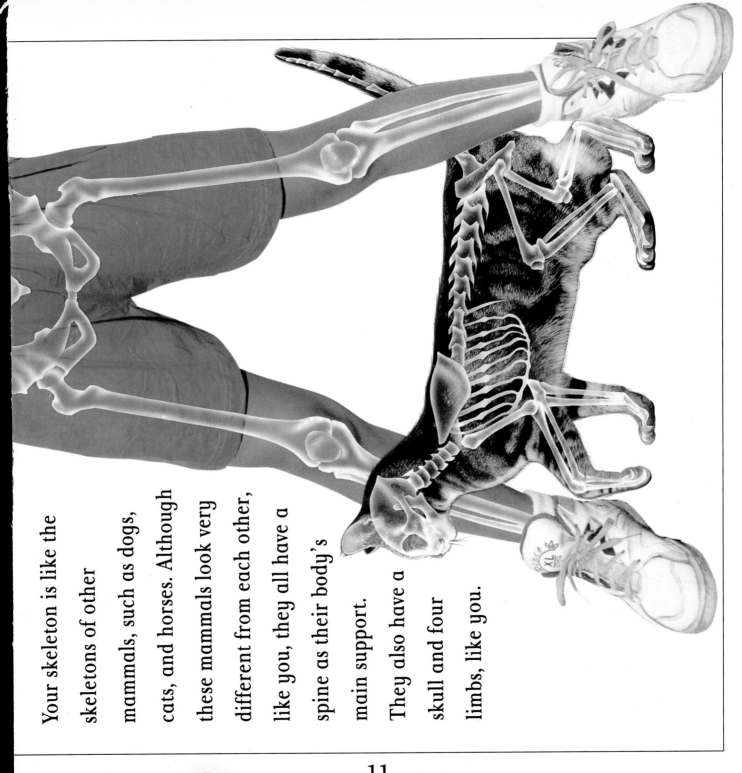

Your skeleton is like the skeletons of other mammals, such as dogs, cats, and horses. Although these mammals look very different from each other, like you, they all have a spine as their body's main support. They also have a skull and four limbs, like you.

The spine

Feel your spine. Is it smooth or knobbly? It feels knobbly because your spine is not one long bone, but a chain of wedge-shaped bones called vertebrae. Vertebrae give your spine extra strength, and also allow you to bend, stretch, and twist.

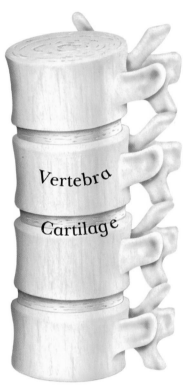

Vertebra

Cartilage

Between the vertebrae there are pads of cartilage, called discs. These are like little cushions of jelly which stop the vertebrae from rubbing against each other.

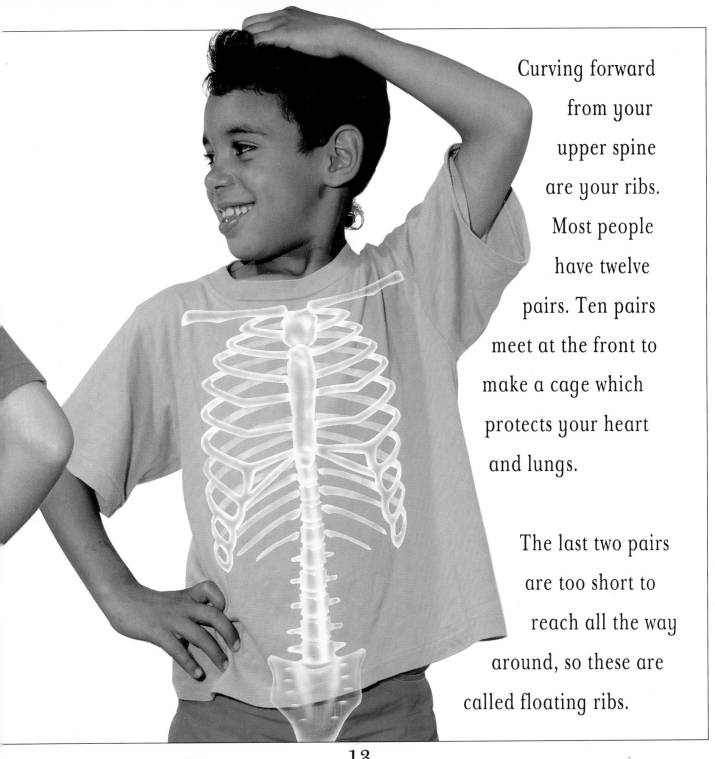

Curving forward from your upper spine are your ribs. Most people have twelve pairs. Ten pairs meet at the front to make a cage which protects your heart and lungs.

The last two pairs are too short to reach all the way around, so these are called floating ribs.

The skull

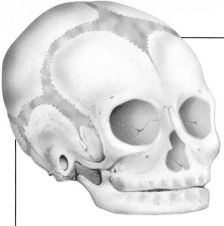

Baby skull

Your skull protects your brain. It is made up of about 30 bones which have grown together to form a kind of helmet.

Until the age of about one, there were spaces between your skull bones. This meant that while you were being born, your skull bones could close up, or even overlap, to make it easier for your head to travel down the birth canal.

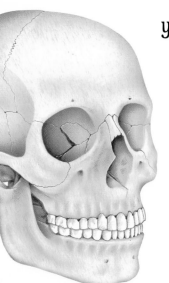

Adult skull

Many bones make up your skull.

The bones of your face protect your eyes and ears. Your eyes are shielded by your forehead and cheekbones. Your delicate inner ears are hidden inside your skull. The smallest bone in your body is found here. It is called the stirrup bone and is only about half as long as a grain of rice – just $1/16$ of an inch (2 millimeters.)

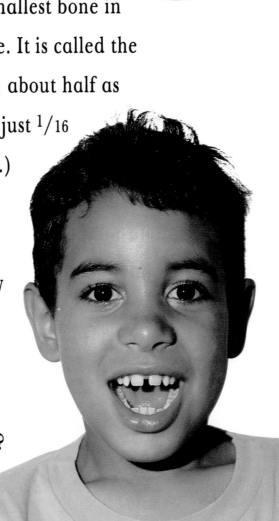

The only skull bone you can move is your lower jaw bone. Your teeth are not made of bone. They are dentine covered in enamel. Count your teeth. How many are baby teeth? How many are grown-up teeth?

Fingers, hands, and arms

Write your name. It's easy isn't it? But only because your hand is made so cleverly! Each hand has 27 bones with three in each finger, and two in each thumb. These bones allow your hand to curve around your pen. Now try writing your name keeping your fingers and thumb straight.

Paint a picture in the air. Watch your hand move up and down at your wrist. Now keep your arm straight and draw a circle in the air. You can do this because the eight bones in your wrist allow you to move your hand almost any way you want.

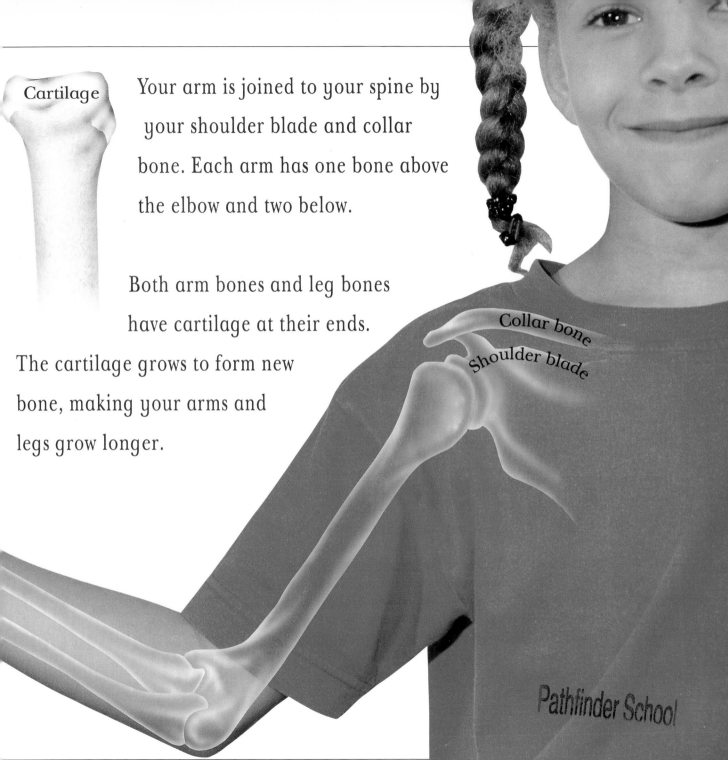

Cartilage

Your arm is joined to your spine by your shoulder blade and collar bone. Each arm has one bone above the elbow and two below.

Both arm bones and leg bones have cartilage at their ends. The cartilage grows to form new bone, making your arms and legs grow longer.

Collar bone

Shoulder blade

Pathfinder School

Legs, feet, and toes

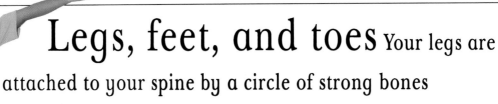

Your legs are attached to your spine by a circle of strong bones called the pelvis. Like your arms, your legs each have three long bones – one above the knee, and two below it.

Your thigh bone is the longest bone in your body. It takes up a quarter of your height – so how long is yours?

Your leg bones need to be very strong to carry the weight of your whole body. Like your arm bones, each leg bone is wider at the ends than at the middle. This gives it extra strength where it joins on to another bone.

Arm bone

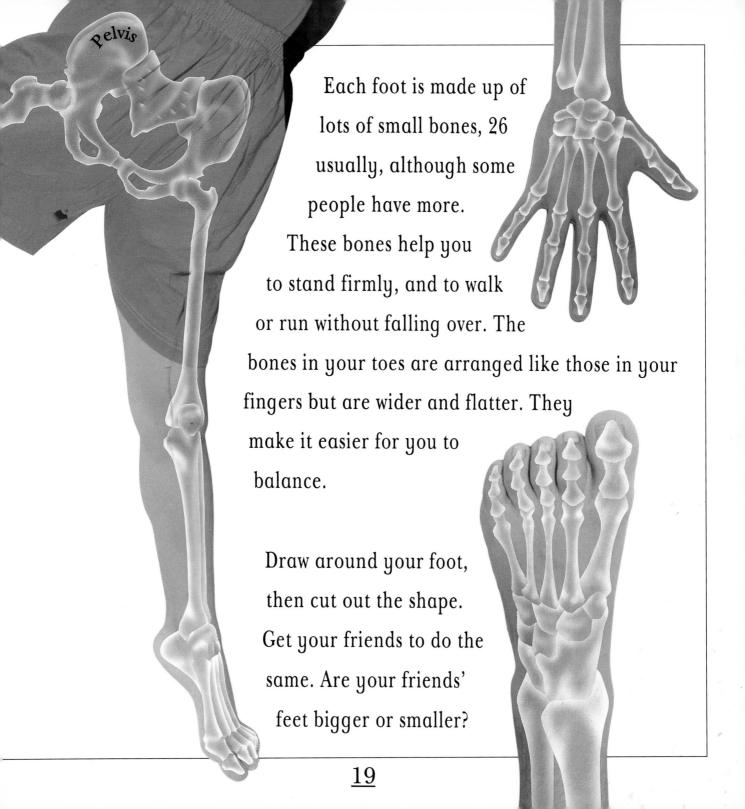

Pelvis

Each foot is made up of lots of small bones, 26 usually, although some people have more. These bones help you to stand firmly, and to walk or run without falling over. The bones in your toes are arranged like those in your fingers but are wider and flatter. They make it easier for you to balance.

Draw around your foot, then cut out the shape. Get your friends to do the same. Are your friends' feet bigger or smaller?

Joints

The place where two bones meet is called a joint. There are fixed joints and moving joints. Fixed joints, such as those in the skull, do not move. Moving joints allow you to bend, twist or turn different parts of your body.

There are two main types of moving joint. Your elbows and knees have hinge joints. They allow your arms and legs to bend and straighten. These joints move in one direction only, like a door hinge.

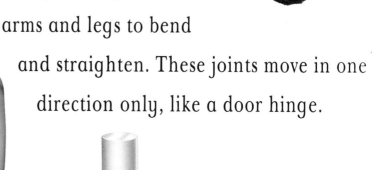

Hinge joint

Hinge joints are also found between the bones in your fingers and toes.

Joints which can move in any direction are called ball and socket joints. These are at your shoulders and hips. Here the rounded end of one bone is held inside a cup-shaped hollow in the other.

Ball and socket joint

All joints are coated with a special fluid, which acts like oil, to help them move. The bones are held in place by strong straps, like rubber bands, called ligaments.

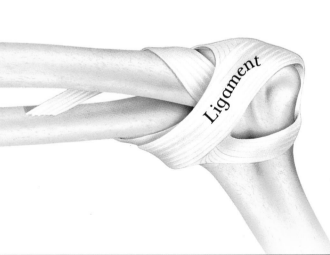

Ligament

Muscles

Every movement you make, however small, is caused by muscles. Some muscles work without your thinking about them – for example, the muscles you use to breathe. Other muscles work when you want them to. If you are going to lift your arm, your brain quickly tells your arm muscles to pull on your arm bones so that they move.

Muscle tensed

Muscles are attached to bones by shiny white bands called tendons. No bones can move on their own.

Muscles work in pairs. When you want to lift an arm, one muscle tenses and shortens to pull up the bone. It then relaxes while another muscle tenses and shortens to straighten the arm again. Muscles can only pull, not push. Place your fingers inside your elbow. Raise your forearm. Can you feel your tendons move?

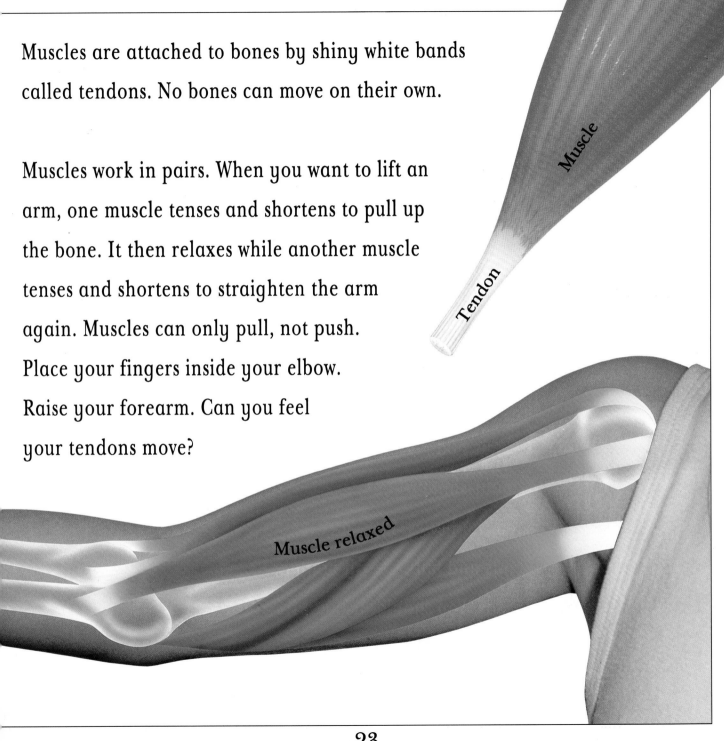

Muscle

Tendon

Muscle relaxed

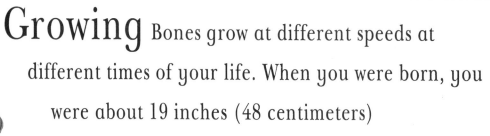

Growing

Bones grow at different speeds at different times of your life. When you were born, you were about 19 inches (48 centimeters) long. At two years old, you were almost twice that length! Between the ages of three and ten, you grow less quickly. After that, growth speeds up again until you stop growing at about the age of 20.

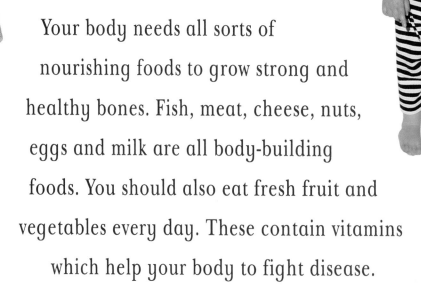

Your body needs all sorts of nourishing foods to grow strong and healthy bones. Fish, meat, cheese, nuts, eggs and milk are all body-building foods. You should also eat fresh fruit and vegetables every day. These contain vitamins which help your body to fight disease.

These are all nutritious foods which you could eat to help you to stay healthy.

How many others can you think of?

Do you try to eat some healthy food every day?

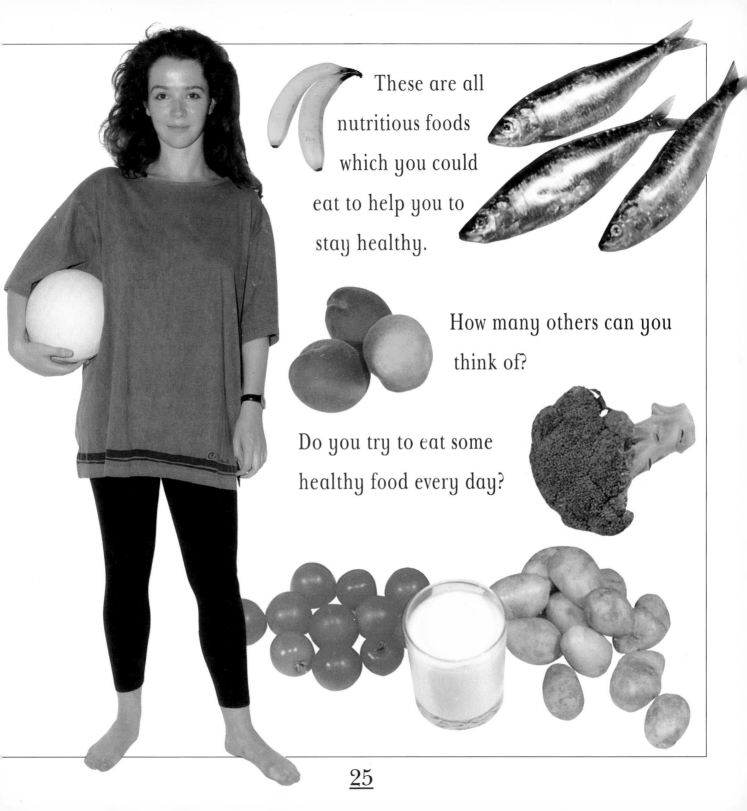

Broken bones

Although a healthy bone is very strong, it can still break. If you hit a bone very hard, or bend a joint too far the wrong way, the bone will snap.

Greenstick fracture

There are different kinds of breaks, or fractures. A greenstick fracture is the least serious because only part of the bone breaks. In a simple fracture, the bone breaks cleanly in two. In a compound fracture, the bone breaks so that part of it pokes through the skin.

Simple fracture

Have you ever broken a bone? Make a chart to show how many of your friends have broken bones. Which ones have they broken? How long did the bones take to heal?

Compound fracture

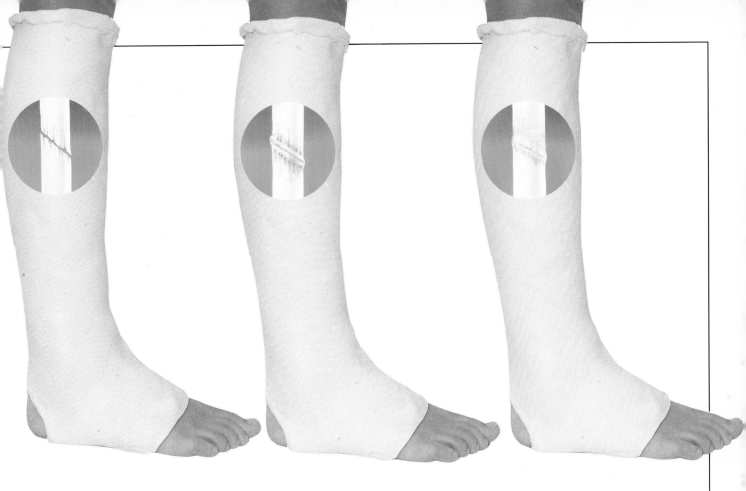

All broken bones mend themselves in the same way. First a blood clot forms to close up the space between the broken ends. The bone cells begin to grow on each side of the break. The cells gradually close the gap with new bone. A plaster cast keeps the pieces in place. It usually takes about twelve weeks for a broken bone to heal.

Did you know?

... that you have the same number of bones in your neck as a giraffe – seven?

... that most girls reach three-quarters of their adult height by the age of seven and a half? Most boys have to wait until they are nine.

... that a baby and a weight-lifter each have the same number of muscles in their body? Over 600 of them!

... that your biggest muscle is the one you sit on?

... that the tallest man in the world, Jan Van Albert, was 9 feet, 5 inches (2.87 meters) tall? He was born in Holland. An American, Robert Wadlow, was 8 feet, 10 inches (2.7 meters) tall. Alam Channa, in the picture, is 8 feet, 2 inches (2.5 meters) tall. He lives in Pakistan.

... that in 24 hours your eye muscles move more than 100,000 times?

INDEX

blood clot 27

bone marrow 8, 9

cartilage 10, 12, 17

cells 9, 27

compact bone 8, 9

floating ribs 13

fracture 26

  compound 26

  greenstick 26

  simple 26

invertebrates 7

joints 20, 21

  ball and socket 21

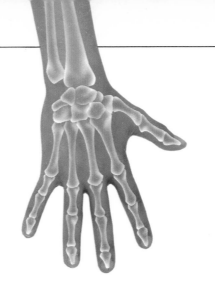

fixed 20

hinge 20

moving 20

ligaments 21

muscles 22, 23, 28, 29

pelvis 18, 19

plaster cast 27

skeleton 6, 8, 10, 11

skull 11, 14, 15, 20

spine 6, 11, 12, 13, 17, 18

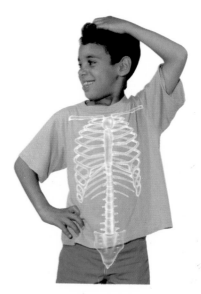

spongy bone 9

stirrup bone 15

tendons 23

vertebrates 6, 7

vitamins 24